WHY TH

SALTY

A TRADITIONAL STORY FROM EUROPE

Many, many years ago,
in a country in Europe,
there lived two little boys.
They were brothers,
and they lived together very happily.

When they grew up,
one brother became very rich,
and the other became very poor.

There came a day
when the poor brother and his wife
had no food and no money.
They were so very hungry,
the poor brother decided
to go and ask his rich brother
for some food.

The rich brother did not want to listen,
but the poor brother begged and begged.
"I'll do anything you command," he pleaded.
"Please, please give us something to eat."

"All right," said the rich brother, angrily.
"Here is a fine leg of ham.
Now I command you
to go far, far away from here —
so far that I will never see you again.
I command you to go and live
in the dark world beneath the earth,
until you can live without having to beg
for my help."

The poor brother was very frightened,
but he had given his word.
And being a very honest man,
he tucked the ham under his arm
and set off for the dark world.

He walked a long way in the darkness,
until he was quite lost.
Suddenly he met a very old,
and very strange, man,
who welcomed him to the underworld.

"Mmm, I can smell ham,"
the old man cackled.
He had not tasted ham
for hundreds of years.
"If you will give me your ham,
I will show you the way out
from this dark underworld,
and as well, I will give you a magic quern.*
This magic quern will bring you
anything that you wish for."

The poor brother was so happy
to be able to return to his home
that he gave the old man the ham.

*A quern is a hand mill used for grinding.

The old man taught him magic words
that would start and stop the quern,
and then he led him from the underworld.
At last, the poor man returned to his home.

"Where have you been?" shouted his wife.
"Where is the food you went to get?
What is that, that you carry with you?"

"Wait and watch," said the poor man.
He set the quern down on the table,
made a wish, and then said
the magic words.
The quern began to grind,
and very soon
it made the finest dinner
that the poor man and his wife
had ever seen.
"We will never be hungry again,"
they said to each other.

They wished for a new
and comfortable home,
and soon it was theirs.
They wished for fine clothes
and money, and they were theirs.
They became very rich.
"We must show our friends
the magic quern,"
they said to each other,
and they did.

The very rich brother
heard the news
and came to see for himself.
"But only a few weeks ago,
you came to me
begging for food," he said.
"How can it be that now
you, too, are a rich man?"

The poor brother
brought out the quern
and made it grind out
all kinds of precious things
to show his brother.

The rich brother was very greedy
and wanted to own the quern.
He came to visit many times, and finally,
one day he tricked his poor brother
into giving it to him to keep.

He took it home and locked it in a room.
Day and night for many years,
he made the quern work for him,
until he lived in a house of gold
and owned the richest treasures
in the world.

One day, a sea captain came to visit.
He had heard of all the treasures
and the house of gold,
and he wanted to see them
with his very own eyes.

Most of all he wanted to see the quern.
"Can it grind out salt?" he asked.

"It can grind out anything you wish,"
said the rich brother.
And he asked the quern
to grind out salt.

The sea captain was tired
of bringing salt from the lands
far beyond the sea.
That night,
he stole the magic quern,
took it to his ship,
and set sail at once.

When he was far away from land,
he put the magic quern on the deck
and commanded it to make salt.
The quern began to grind out salt.
It worked and worked
until the ship's hold was full of salt.

The sea captain
did not know the magic words
to stop the quern from working.
It kept on making more and more salt,
until the ship was so loaded with salt
that it sank to the bottom of the sea.

Stories say that the quern is grinding there to this very day,
and that is why the sea is salty.